# WHEN THE
# Saints Go Marching Abroad

Peter Frederick Harling

Grosvenor House
Publishing Limited

All rights reserved
Copyright © Peter Frederick Harling, 2021

The right of Peter Frederick Harling to be identified as the author of this
work has been asserted in accordance with Section 78
of the Copyright, Designs and Patents Act 1988

The book cover is copyright to Peter Frederick Harling

This book is published by
Grosvenor House Publishing Ltd
Link House
140 The Broadway, Tolworth, Surrey, KT6 7HT.
www.grosvenorhousepublishing.co.uk

This book is sold subject to the conditions that it shall not, by way of
trade or otherwise, be lent, resold, hired out or otherwise circulated
without the author's or publisher's prior consent in any form of binding or
cover other than that in which it is published and
without a similar condition including this condition being imposed
on the subsequent purchaser.

A CIP record for this book
is available from the British Library

ISBN 978-1-83975-565-1

# Preface By Nick Beal

Nicholas "Nick" David Beal was a rugby union full back for Northampton Saints, England and the British & Ireland Lions.

Since his retirement from professional rugby in 2004 Nick is now a financial advisor for the Northampton firm David Williams IFA and retains his passion for the game as a non-executive director of the Saints.

"I personally have been lucky enough to experience playing and watching rugby on many different levels. From my early childhood years when my parents ferried me around the country for various matches, through to me standing on the touchline watching my own two sons playing this great game."

"The years went by and the game turned professional, whilst the stadiums got bigger and so did the crowds, the same camaraderie continued both on and off the field. I am confident that my parents felt that all of the time they had invested in enabling me to play from a young age, was all worthwhile."

"The away trips that they have made to games with friends over many years have not always been successful from a results perspective, but there is no doubt that they enjoyed every single one of them (well, apart from when I broke my leg at Vicarage Road!). Whatever the result, they were always to be found in the bar after a game having a drink or two with fellow Saints, England, or Lions supporters as well as `opposition fans".

"The highlight, I am sure, was the time spent in South Africa with the Lions in 1997. One of my many memories of this two-month tour was not only seeing the smiles on my parents faces as they travelled around the country enjoying the rugby and experiencing the different local cultures, but of also seeing the joy on thousands of travelling Lions fans. This to me summed up the enjoyment of travelling to rugby games. It forms a bond with fellow fans which at times can become tribe like. It enables you to travel to places where you may not ordinarily go and meet the locals who are always as welcoming as they can be"

"I know that the support of fans that any team gets makes a huge difference to on-field performance. When coupled with the great time that can be had on away trips, I say that you have no excuses – get out there and follow your team!"

# Acknowledgements

This book is only possible with the support and dedication of the people who have been involved in the various trips. I am very lucky to have such long standing pals that have participated and the comradeship it has generated.

It would normally be unfair to pick out individuals but two of our loyal and committed participants have passed away but I am sure they have subscribed to BT Sport Heaven.

## Alan Hunter 1948 – 2013

Alan was everything you would want on a tour - lively, supportive, outrageous at times, always helpful and by his character the initiative behind many of the amusing side stories. It was a major shock to all concerned when Alan passed away after a short illness

## Graham Bose 1961 – 2019

Graham was one of the original travellers being my room-mate on the trip to Biarritz. He was always one of the first to sign up for foreign trips.

He was well liked by all who met him and was an enthusiastic Saints supporter and active sportsman. He was hoping to see the Saints play in Romania but in the end cancer won.

THEY WILL BE GREATLY MISSED

# Forward

The game Rugby Union is a unique sport watched throughout the world by a broad cross-section of the population. On the pitch the players (or should I say Gladiators) endure physical impacts for 80 minutes where your average human being would probably take the remaining 79 minutes to recover from the first minute's encounters.

Despite the intense physicality on the pitch there are two golden rules that have endured the sands of time even with the advent of the professional era, the increased focus on commercialism, increased financial rewards, the investment in ever improving stadiums and extensive media coverage –

1) The referee is always correct even when some of the crowd try to help him when he is obviously misguided. The introduction of TV replays and the ability to use the "yellow card" (10 minutes in the sin bin) provide the referee with a bit of armoury as and when required.
2) During the match the intense rivalry between the players in pursuit of that scoring opportunity is paramount, but as soon as that electronic clock reaches 80 minutes the players warmly thank the opposition for beating nine bells out of each other and buy each other a pint or ten in the bar.

Coupled with this ethos, the crowd also have rules to follow –

a) In a civilised stadium there is deadly silence for what seems an eternity whilst the fly half goes through his unique approach to place kicking.
b) The use of obscene language is frowned upon and could result in the perpetrator seeking an alternative venue to watch the remainder of the match.

But the real unique factor about rugby union is the fact that one can sit next to a supporter of the opposition team, exchange pleasantries before and during the match and shake hands warmly regardless of the result of the game.

So where does this perfect backdrop emerge from?? Well I believe it stems from the grass roots of the game. When you have spent every Sunday morning standing on a touch line watching your son (or daughter) become blue with cold and muddier than a hippopotamus wallowing in a muddy pitch like at Welford Road, you are bound to question your own sanity. Then the light comes on and you remember that the game is character forming, healthy exercise, team-work, discipline enforcement and ultimately comrade building. I also believe the kids get something from it too, not just the dads fighting to get to the bar for that pint of the black stuff or two and a J2O and bag of chips for the lad (in my case).

The pinnacle of this education process is the annual "dads and sons" away trip which justifies 25 prime-of-life men (pseudonym for past-it) behaving irresponsibly whilst their youngsters, who should be tucked in bed getting a good night's sleep before the match, are crammed into one bedroom trying to break the code for the "education" channel on the TV.

The report on the trip for the club news sheet includes the statement (...and I'm afraid that is another Holiday Inn that we are no longer welcome.)

## Objective of this book

Having set the scene for the potential readership then, this book is the ultimate handbook for those supporters who fancy a weekend away in a European city with like-minded enthusiasts of the game who like to engage in culture (pop into a cathedral), retail therapy (e.g. buy a set of table napkins, which aren't needed, as a peace-offering), watch the match of course and sample the local cuisine being sure at all times to maintain a reasonable level of fluid intake to counteract the effect of singing etc.

The book will take you through all the stages from planning to execution of the trip including where to book, how to get there, ways to reduce costs (but not compromise quality), details of the stadium etc. It concludes with a travel log of the cities we have visited detailing where to go, things to do, places to see, restaurants to try and most important – where the Irish bar is and other worthwhile refreshment houses.

# Contents

| | | |
|---|---|---|
| 1 | Background and Credibility | 1 |
| 2 | Getting the Team Together | 6 |
| 3 | Getting Started | 9 |
| 4 | Making Choices | 10 |
| | a. Travel | 10 |
| | b. Hotels | 10 |
| | c. Match Tickets | 11 |
| 5 | Contingency Planning | 12 |
| 6 | Trip to Romania | 15 |
| 7 | Venue Information | 20 |
| 8 | Lions, Six Nations & World Cup | 60 |
| 9 | Places We Haven't Yet Visited | 65 |
| 10 | Top 10 Irish Bars | 69 |
| 11 | Memorable Occasions | 72 |
| 12 | Post Trip Review and Report | 73 |
| 13 | Summary and Conclusion | 75 |
| Appendices | | 76 |
| | 1 Flight Finder | 76 |
| | 2 Northampton Saints-Record in Europe | 79 |
| | 3 Cities Stayed and Clubs Played | 80 |
| | 4 Additional Grounds | 81 |

# Chapter 1

# Background and Credibility

## Justification

During the past 18 years I have arranged 53 trips for fellow rugby supporters. As you may have realised by now our team is Northampton Saints. I have been a season ticket holder for over 2 decades.

The Saints have enjoyed reasonable success in Europe with a win in 2000 and runners-up in 2012. We also lifted the secondary prize – The Challenge Cup twice.

It might easily be argued that it is easy to follow a winning team but the players and staff of teams that have been successful would also argue that the away support they get motivates them to win.

The atmosphere in foreign stadium can be very intimidating but that little corner of the ground with Northampton supporters waving their flags and singing their hearts out encourages the players to greater things. So come on you folk who support English premiership teams – get out there and have some fun.

## You have a Choice

Most if not all English Premiership clubs organise trips to European (and some domestic) venues and do it well. Whilst I naturally favour the DIY version, I try below to provide a balanced pros and cons for each approach.

Firstly the club package – on the plus side the club take most of the risk, worry or even just the effort. However that comes at a premium and from our extensive experience that frequently doubles the cost for equivalent components.

On the other hand the DIY approach clearly saves considerable expense (which in my case justifies two weekends away per year on a two for the price of one basis). Also the DIY approach has the following additional benefits –

- Flexibility – you decide every component of the trip
- Choice – you select and negotiate hotels, where you travel from and with which carrier or even which mode is best
- If time allows what excursions you might include
- Premium choice of match tickets

But I acknowledge that at first this may feel daunting and therefore for your first trip you may opt for the club option

## The Numbers Game

To illustrate our experience and capability of the "tried and tested formula" it is interesting to reflect some statistics from our tours.

- Costs – The average costs achieved to date for the main components is as follows –
  - Average hotel room cost per night is £35.18
  - Average cost per flight £41.36

- People – As previously mentioned at the time of writing this book, we had completed 53 trips.
  - The average length of stay was 1.89 nights
  - 24 people were involved which included a loyal base of 10 people who accounted for 81% of the weighted attendance.

- The youngest was a mere 11 months old (young Oliver had to endure sub-zero temperatures in Treviso)
- Two people were over 65 years old at the time of travel.
- The average attendance was 4.89, highest 9 and the lowest being 2

Hotels – In order to accommodate everyone I had to book 478 beds in 66 hotels. Mostly twin rooms but 2 cases of double for 2 guys (the reason and solution to this heterosexual nightmare will be revealed later in the book)

Transport – The most common approach to most venues is by plane

    Airlines – Ryanair    24
                  Easyjet     18
                  Flybe       10
                  Aer Lingus  4

Others (2 flights each) British Airways, Air France, Buzz, Monarch, Thomson Fy, MyTravelLite

Trains – these were used in three ways

1) As the primary mode (6) - e.g. Glasgow

2) In conjunction with flying (2) - e.g. Castres – train from Toulouse

3) For excursions (15) - e.g. day trip to Marseilles from Toulon

Hire Cars – As with trains these were required in conjunction with flying or for specific excursions –

e.g. for the Agen game we flew into Toulouse, used the hire car to get to Agen but on the day after the match we did a day trip to Bordeaux

We mainly used Hertz (7) but also used Enterprise (2), Avis (1) and Basic (1)

Ferry –   Only once on a trip to Eire

Coach –   Only once on a trip to Cardiff although coaches and buses were required e.g. transfer from airport to hotel/town

Executive Minibus – for the 2$^{nd}$ trip to Treviso we caught an Easyjet flight into Venice Marco Polo and hired a specialist executive transfer company to cover the 30miles between airport and hotel

And finally (particularly trips in England and Wales) use of own car where practical.

One of the key requirements is to negotiate best times and cheapest rates. The message here is if you get in soonest you stand a chance of saving a bob or two.

## Summary of Chapter 1

The major objective of this chapter is to establish credibility and hence reassure you we have extensive knowledge and have learnt a few tricks along the way. It is worth stating that we are not qualified travel agents nor do we claim to be the absolute cheapest, but we constantly beat the more commercial operations (see chapter 8 on Lions Tours).

As a disclaimer I would state that the following applies –

1) We do not make money – we charge whatever it costs
2) We do not guarantee this as the only solution – there is always more than one way to skin a moggy

3) We provide lots of practical advice in this book which we hope will minimise individual financial costs, but you know your pals (or perhaps you discover some home truths).

At this stage I throw out a challenge – if there is someone out there that can claim and demonstrate that they have arranged more tours for rugby weekends then please email me peter.harling@nortonexecutive.com and we will compare notes over a shandy or two.

# Chapter 2

# Getting the Team Together

You may have already discussed the possibility with some friends or have been inspired by this book, either way a team is required. However, you, could start with just two of you, but 4-6 is ideal.

Long before the fixture announced there are a number of aspects worth tackling –

Check Availability – who is up for it in principle

**The European Champions Cup** – the weekends will be known well in advance. Assuming your team is A then typically the schedule is –

ROUND 1 – Team A   2$^{nd}$ weekend October Home or way
ROUND 2 – Team B   3$^{rd}$ weekend October Reverse of Round 1
ROUND 3 – Team C   2$^{nd}$ weekend December Home or Away
ROUND 4 – Team C   3$^{rd}$ Weekend December Reverse of Round 3
ROUND 5 – Team B   2$^{nd}$ weekend January Reverse of Round 2
ROUND 6 – Team A   3$^{rd}$ Weekend January Reverse of Round 1

There is no significance in the order A/B/C which might be influenced by the TV. The TV companies seem to play a significant part in deciding kick-off times.

The three home ties are not relevant as it is assumed that these will be covered by season tickets, which won't involve an over-night stay.

There is some degree of seeding – keeping the big boys apart, but at this stage all we can do is to blank out those weekend and check availability from your team.

Recently the group stage changed to five groups of 4 teams (it was 6 groups of 4) with the group winners and the best three 2nd places progressing in to the quarterfinals.

**The European Challenge Cup** – The second tier competition has a similar structure with only the group winners progressing to their quarter final.

If you are feeling very ambitious you may also get the members of team to indicate which are their no-go weekends due to prior commitments or available holiday entitlement.

You may also be able to ascertain whether they wished to or could afford to be part of all or more than one trip.

NB – in World Cup years then Rounds 1&2 are scheduled in the middle weekends in November.

This 2nd tier competition effectively doubles the scope for rugby tours.

The bookings must be tied to a specific person. If someone wishes or has to cancel their participation then it's only fair that they are accountable for those costs that cannot be recovered.

If subsequently someone else wishes to join the tour then they could take over some of the costs, but the tickets and any administration fee is down to the original person.

1) As a policy we keep costs down by booking twin bedrooms. So if we have an odd number in the team then one of two things

happen. If someone particularly wants the single room then they have to pay the higher rate. If not then we draw lots or "spoof" to decide who but also we equalise the rates so everyone pays the same rate.
2) As a rule we aim for 3 star or better in an optimal location with respect to the stadium but more particular the bars and restaurants – value for money is the objective.
3) When on tour we operate a kitty system designed to operate when everyone is together. If for any reason the group gets split the kitty is temporarily suspended.
4) During the trip we employ a gentleman's agreement – "What happens on tour stays on tour". (This is generally upheld until 10 years later someone writes a book about it).

At this point, before the "sexism police" swoop down on me I would like to qualify and clarify the situation regarding BOY/GIRL. Whilst it is true that historically the constitution of the team has been predominantly male, this is not a precursor for future trips. indeed more latterly the Husband/Wife entity is a significant component. Not to lose the true essence of a RUGBY trip the following guidelines seem pragmatic –

1) Beer will be consumed by the pint. Ladies are allowed to have halves but no cherries or umbrellas

2) Singing of songs which hint that women are objects of desire rather than the people who sanction the trip (Yes its true – some of the guys have to get a signed chitty before declaring availability)

3) The consumption of a pint of Guinness or two with a full English breakfast prior to your flight to your destination is an important and treasured ritual.

NB – please substitute your nationality as appropriate if you are a non-English citizen

# Chapter 3

# Getting Started

The following sequence of events are essential components of a successful tour.

1) The team leader has the responsibility of finding out when the draw for the group stages is to be announced and communicating it to potential tourists. At this stage all you can do is to find out who might be interested.

2) In the few weeks between (1) and (3) the tour leader works out the various alternatives and is in regular contact with the potential tourists checking the various alternatives. It is vital in this period that passport and additional personal data is collated so that flights can be booked simultaneously.

3) A few weeks later the actual match details are announced and flights can be booked and the package can start to evolve. This is a crucial activity and the speed of booking flights can reduce the cost considerably.

4) Clearly the cost of flights is initially down to one person but the expectation is that individuals reimburse the funder immediately.

# Chapter 4

# Making Choices

The great advantage of doing it yourself is that you can chose many of the parameters.

1. **Travel** – for many of the venues flights are the obvious answer. However there are situations that may require a more creative approach –

    a. No flights from UK to appropriate town/city e.g. Castres where the solution might be flight to one of half a dozen nearby airports and then hire car, train or coach to the venue

    b. For personal home location variances or duration availability it might make sense for one or more participants to travel separately

    c. Getting to the airport might be by car for some of the team or train/coach for others

2. **Hotels** – Ideally we all stay at the same hotel but there are situations where an alternative solution is required -

    a. As previously stated, as a matter of principle, we arrange twin rooms. However if there is an odd number or someone has a desire for a single room. In the case of the latter the specifier picks up the additional costs

    b. If someone joins the team later and there is no availability at the chosen hotel then an alternative needs to found

3. **Match Tickets** – It makes sense and is important for enabling vocal clusters of supporters that we all situations together. The situation that might challenge this wisdom are –

    a. Tickets purchased from the club, this is safest and easiest

    b. Tickets purchased on the internet from competitor website. This can be slightly cheaper and much better seats as the website thinks you're a home supporter

NB – Be careful with the last choice as it can catapult you onto the distribution list of some obscure French website. I have been trying to get rid of www.usap.cat for ages.

# Chapter 5

# Contingency Planning

· ● ● ● ·

The old saying "If it could go wrong it probably will" is very true and of course the more trips you do the greater the probability. So let's look at common issues and how to mitigate them. Below I list the common issues that can occur and some solutions. This list is not exhaustive but it gives you a checklist

POTENTIAL TRAVEL ISSUE

1) Problems getting to airport on time due to car breakdown, journey time extended due to accident or roadworks. This is even more critical if the party is split into two or more groups. The golden rule is always leave enough time. If however it does occur then those on time must catch the flight and those delayed must seek alterative flights (at extra cost and time). The tour leader may be able to help plan an alternative.

2) Delay in airport security/passport control resulting in arriving at the gate too late. If it looks likely make sure you are assertive and inform security staff – they will usually fast-track you to the front.

3) Forgetting your flight documents, Passport and Boarding Passes. The latter is easily retrievable. The forgetful person could get a replacement at a very high charge or may be bailed out by his ever-diligent tour leader who by chance had a duplicate set of boarding passes. So the former has to weigh up the options which may be to miss the tour altogether "he's gone

for an early bath" to quote the late, great Eddie Waring whilst the latter is in line for a tour forfeit (usually a round of drinks).

4) Flight delayed or cancelled by airline or air traffic control. This is a tricky one to mitigate for. The airlines will endeavour to find alternatives for you, but the reality is these budget airlines tend to have only one flight a day.

5) Lost luggage – we avoid this possible issue by making a golden rule – cabin bags only. This has two additional benefits – you save on airline charges which could be £20+ per flight, but also you are one of the first to queue for hire car, bus or taxi. The only potential challenge is to remember that extra value 200ml bottle of Head & Shoulders (with added coconut essence) will probably be confiscated along with your favourite Manchester United branded corkscrew. Not sure what airport security do with all the offensive corkscrews, but take a look at the hair of the staff – no dandruff to be seen.

6) Weather issues – most of the matches are played in the Autumn/Wintertime and therefore it is remarkable that bad weather is not as prevalent as it could be. There are two aspects to consider –

   a. Weather causing difficulties in travelling to the venue. The worst are fog and snow. This especially becomes problematic if you have a long journey from airport to venue. The by-word here is safety first. If it looks dangerous then pull off the road and if necessary, find a nearby hotel.

   b. Causing match to be cancelled or moved due to one or more of the following –

      I. Frozen pitch
      II. Waterlogged pitch
      III. Snow

IV. Fog

V. Extremely high winds

7) Match moved for TV requirements

TRUE STORY

In December 2009 we were due to play Treviso. The night before the match the forecast was clear skies and mild although there was a hint of snow.

The next morning we awoke to a foot of snow transferring the landscape to a winter-wonder-land. A few of us went to the ground after breakfast to find an army of people and machines clearing the snow. By a miracle the match went ahead.

NB The home team have an obligation to provide an alternate arrangement. This can lead to last minute changes.

*Touch wood, Harling Tours have never lost a team member although on one of our earlier trips (to Biarritz) one of our team lost his way in the Irish Bar whilst getting a round in. He decided to position himself near the door with his tray of 5 pints of Guinness and a diet Coke for the lady. His logic was "they have to come this way eventually" was sound but in the meantime, he thought it was silly to waste the beer – 5 empty glasses but at least the Coke had been spared. Our teammate needed some guidance on the way to the hotel and struggled to make breakfast. We have an unrecorded rule – You must make breakfast after a night on the pop.*

# Chapter 6

# The Trip to Romania

When the groups were announced (mid 2018) I was excited to see the name Timisoara alongside Clermont and Newport. Not that I was dismissive of the latter two places, but we had visited them in the past and I instinctively knew there would be a lukewarm reaction to another trip to Clermont (Newport does not require an overnight stay and hence is outside the scope of this book).

Following my formula, the first thing to do is to is ascertain who is interested and gain their commitment to the trip. I was encouraged to find that three others were equally enthusiastic.

## Research for the Trip

This trip required more planning than usual due to the complexity of the language, currency and the lack of experience of dealing with an eastern bloc country. However, research did throw up an interesting opportunity – if we were to catch the 7:30am train from Timisoara to Budapest we would have a good 24 hours in a great city before flying back to Stansted on the 15:50 Ryanair flight from Budapest. The added complication was the fact that the Czech Republic company that operates the railway wouldn't commit to the times and cost of the journey until the new timetable was to be published on 1st December. On that date, I spoke to a lady and placed an order and was encouraged to receive a FED EX delivery with 4 tickets/seat reservation.

## Outbound Flight

The next task was to find the best way to get there. We found that Ryanair flew to Timisoara from Bergamo (Milan in Ryanair speak). We could get to Bergamo from Stansted again with Ryanair.

The match was to be played 15/12 so we booked flights as follows –

Depart Stansted 13.40 arrive Milan 16.35 1hr 55m flight time

Depart Milan 19.25 arrive Timisoara 22.10 1hr 45m flight time

The outbound flights cost £70

## Arrival in Romania (14th December)

Unbeknown to us about 5.00pm local time it started to snow (big time) so that by the time we landed the snow was several inches thick and still coming down. Fortunately, we had arranged with the hotel to pick us up and we had an interesting journey to the hotel – the Romanians are obviously used to snowy conditions.

## Casa del Sol

The hotel was splendid (Casa del Sol) and the staff were very supportive – they opened the bar and the first round of drinks was complimentary.

Hotel cost 3 nights B&B £110.14 (£36.71 per night)

# Timisoara Map

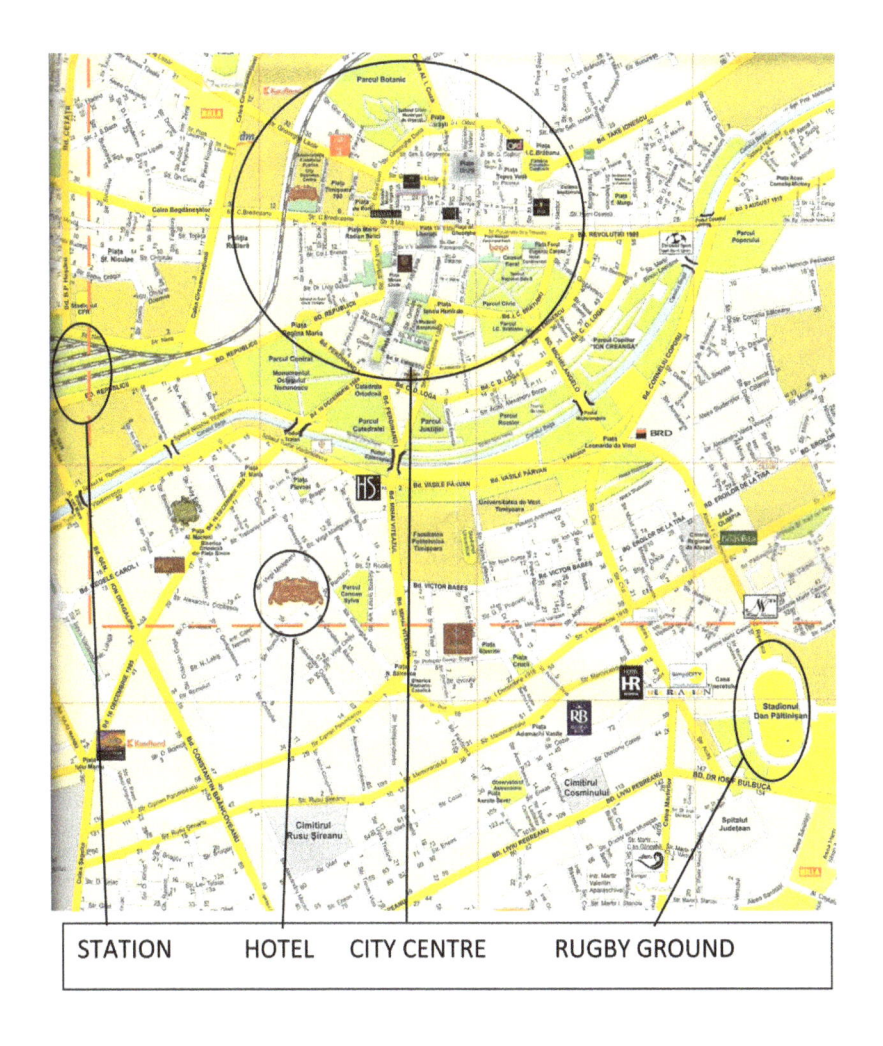

STATION   HOTEL   CITY CENTRE   RUGBY GROUND

The hotel was ideally central for all our requirements, an excellent restaurant and a swimming pool (although you would have to break the ice to enjoy it).

## The Day of the Match

Supporters and players at a snow bound ground in Timisoara.

Although the outcome was inevitable, curiosity got the better of us and we piled into a taxi and went to the ground. We arrived at the same time as the Club group – I estimated about 100 supporters had made the trip. An army of locals were fighting a losing battle trying to clear the pitch (it transpired that this "army" was in fact convicts from the prison)

The Club group were due to fly back after 2 nights in a hotel but were busy trying to arrange extra accommodation as attempts to kick-start the plane had failed.

## The Journey to Budapest

The extra trip by train (cost £54.67) proved to be inspirational although yet again there was a twist in events – the train stopped in the middle of nowhere for 2 hours with no explanation. Nevertheless we still got quality time in Budapest – a beautiful city and well worth a longer visit.

A slight disappointment was the hotel, but it was economical at £20 B&B.

The total costs for travel and accommodation - £290.14.

When we add in cost for meals, beers, taxis and travel to and from airport the whole trip was about £430. Not bad for a 5 day trip and about half the Club package pro-rata, no rugby, but an enjoyable and interesting trip.

**TIP – Szimpla Kert.** A very unique bar well worth a visit

Kazinczy utca 14, Budapest 1075

Phone - +36 20 261 8669

# Chapter 7

# Venue Information

## VENUE PROFILES

### FRANCE

| | |
|---|---|
| Agen | 25 |
| Bezier | 26 |
| Biarritz | 27 |
| Bayonne | 29 |
| Bordeaux | 29 |
| Castres | 30 |
| Albi | 31 |
| Clermont | 32 |
| Grenoble | 32 |
| Lyon | 33 |
| Montpellier | 34 |
| Paris | 35 |
| Perpignan | 36 |
| Toulon | 39 |
| Nice | 40 |
| Toulouse | 41 |

### SPAIN

| | |
|---|---|
| San Sebastian | 43 |
| BILbao | 43 |

### ITALY

| | |
|---|---|
| Parma | 44 |
| Treviso | 45 |
| Verona | 47 |

### IRELAND

| | |
|---|---|
| Belfast | 48 |
| Galway | 48 |
| Dublin | 49 |
| Limerick | 51 |

### SCOTLAND

| | |
|---|---|
| Glasgow | 53 |
| Edinburgh | 54 |

### WALES

| | |
|---|---|
| Cardiff/Newport | 55 |
| Swansea/Llanelli | 56 |

### ENGLAND

| | |
|---|---|
| Exeter | 57 |
| Manchester/Leeds | 58 |
| Newcastle/Plymouth | 58 |
| St.Ives | 59 |

## EXCURSIONS

| | |
|---|---|
| WEST PYRENEES | 28 |
| EAST PYRENEES | 37 |
| COLLIOURE | 38 |
| MARSEILLE | 40 |
| CITE DE L'ESPACE | 42 |
| VENICE | 46 |
| HOWTH/MALAHIND | 50 |
| GREYSTONES/BRAY | 50 |
| BUNRATTY CASTLE | 52 |
| S W EIRE | 52 |

## Our Supporters

One of the many positives about following your team abroad is the fellow supporters you meet and the friendship that follows. Curiously, for some bizarre reason, the people you meet on tour you rarely see at home games but as you walk round the place of the match you give a knowing nod of the head (which means we had a beer or two in that bar in Toulouse but neither of us can remember the other's name).

## Home Team Supporters

Equally the response from the home supporters is always welcoming but always touched by the disbelief that these guys have travelled 1000 miles to watch a rugby match.

This congeniality continues up to the start of the match when for 80 minutes tribal warfare takes over and both sets of fans direct their passions towards the guys on the pitch. Strangely the French supporters do not always agree with the referee. At the final whistle no matter what the outcome you spontaneously embrace all of the home supporters nearby or in the bar.

## Your Team

The players really appreciate your support and acknowledge that at the end of the match.

Frequently in the evening they are allowed out and find where the fans are at play and have a beer or two and an insight into their views on life or learn new rugby songs.

# French Teams and their Location

Although European rugby competitions are held with Top 14, we provide teams as at the 2015-2016 season from both Top 14 and Pro Division 2 leagues so that we cover changes with promotion and relegation. For example, it is not long ago that Biarritz and Perpignan were challenging for the Heineken cup at the knockout stages.

You will no doubt realise that professional rugby union is based in the south with only the two Paris teams in the north.

# AGEN (LOT-ET-GARONNE)

| CLUBNAME | S U Agen | STADIUM | Stade Armandie |
|---|---|---|---|
| ADDRESS | 19 Rue Pierre de Coucertin, 47000, Agen, Lot-et-Garonne | | |
| WEBSITE | www.agen-rugby.com | CAPACITY | 14,000 |

Agen presents a logistical challenge as it has not got a commercial airport. The choice is –
1) Rail station plus train journey to Agen (direction Bordeaux) or hire car to Agen
2) Flight to Bordeux then similar choices re train/hire car.

The choice will influenced by –
a) Number of team (e.g. 5 is a car full)
b) Timing of inter-connecting transport
c) Opportunity of using the hire car to explore other places of interest (we hired a car and did a day trip to Bordeaux from Agen)
d) Cost of chosen route. For Agen we are in no doubt where to stay – the Chateau des Jacobans is 4 star luxury at 3 star prices and in city

Highly Rated:

Chateau Jacobins

# BEZIER (HERAULT)

| CLUBNAME | Asb Bezier Herault | STADIUM | Stade des Mediterranee | |
|---|---|---|---|---|
| ADDRESS | Avenue des Olympiads, 34500, Beziers | | | |
| WEBSITE | www.asbh.net | | CAPACITY | 18,500 |

Bezier currently play in the second tier of french rugby so it is unlikely in the forseeable future that they will be drawn in the premier european competions. However they are financialy well backed and ambitious as demonstrtated by their impressive stadium.

The city does have an international airport and does provide an alternative entry point to this corner of France especially as the economic flight operators use this airport.

The city is built on high ground with the impressive 12$^{th}$ century bridge – Pont Vieux dominating the river Orb valley.

The city itself is compact and centred around the 12$^{th}$ century cathedral – St. Nazaire

# BIARRITZ (PYRENEES-ATLANTIQUES)

| CLUBNAME | Biarritz Olympique | STADIUM | Parc des Sport d'Aquilera | |
|---|---|---|---|---|
| ADDRESS | Rue Cino del Duca 64200, Biarritz, Pays Basque | | | |
| WEBSITE | www.bo-pb.com | CAPACITY | 13,500 | |

Biarritz is a great place to spend a weekend. The small airport is very close to the town and a 10 minute local bus ride has you soon checking in at your hotel.' Biarritz is only 10 miles from the spanish border so it is truly Basque in many ways.

Biarritz is the surfing capital of Europe with giant Atlantic waves being funnelled into this corner of the Bay of Biscay. Don't forget to pack your ironing board so as not to miss the big rollers.

The huge sandy beach is fronted by classy buildings such as the Hotel du Palais and the magnificent casino.

On match day allow 20 minutes to walk to the ground. Get there early to enjoy the pre-match culinery offerings. In the evening make sure you visit the Irish pub and Pascal Ondart's bar.

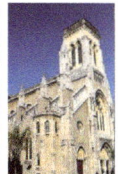

Highly Rated:
Pascal Ondarts
Hotel Florida
L'escurial

# Excursion 1 from Biarritz - Western Pyrenees

If you have a spare day in your itinerary, then you may want to consider this excursion. The route takes you to a height of 1573 metres with some fantastic views and sights on the way. However, it would be unwise to undertake this if there is any chance snow or poor visibility.

WHEN THE SAINTS GO MARCHING ABROAD

# Excursion 2 from BIARRITZ – BAYONNE

| CLUBNAME | Aviron Bayonne | STADIUM | Stade Jean Dauger |
|---|---|---|---|
| ADDRESS | 8 Avenue Femand Forgues, 64100 Bayonne |||
| WEBSITE | www.abrugby.com | CAPACITY | 16,934 |

Bayonne is approximately five miles from Biarritz and the two cities are connected by a local bus. Bayonne is worth a trip if only to see the splendour of Bayonne Cathedral.

# Excursion from AGEN – BORDAEUX

| CLUBNAME | Bordeaux Begles | STADIUM | Stade Chaban-Delmas |
|---|---|---|---|
| ADDRESS | 25 Rue Delfín Loche, 33130, Begles |||
| WEBSITE | www.ubbrugby.com | CAPACITY | 34,263 |

Bordaeux is an hours drive north of Agen and the stadium is in a region called Begles. Bordaeux has a wealth of historic buildings and plenty of restaurants and bars.

# CASTRES (TARN)

| CLUBNAME | Castres Olympique | STADIUM | Stade Pierre-Antoine | |
|---|---|---|---|---|
| ADDRESS | Rue de Bisseouss, 81100, Castres, Tarn | | | |
| WEBSITE | www.castres-olympique.fr | CAPACITY | 11,500 | |

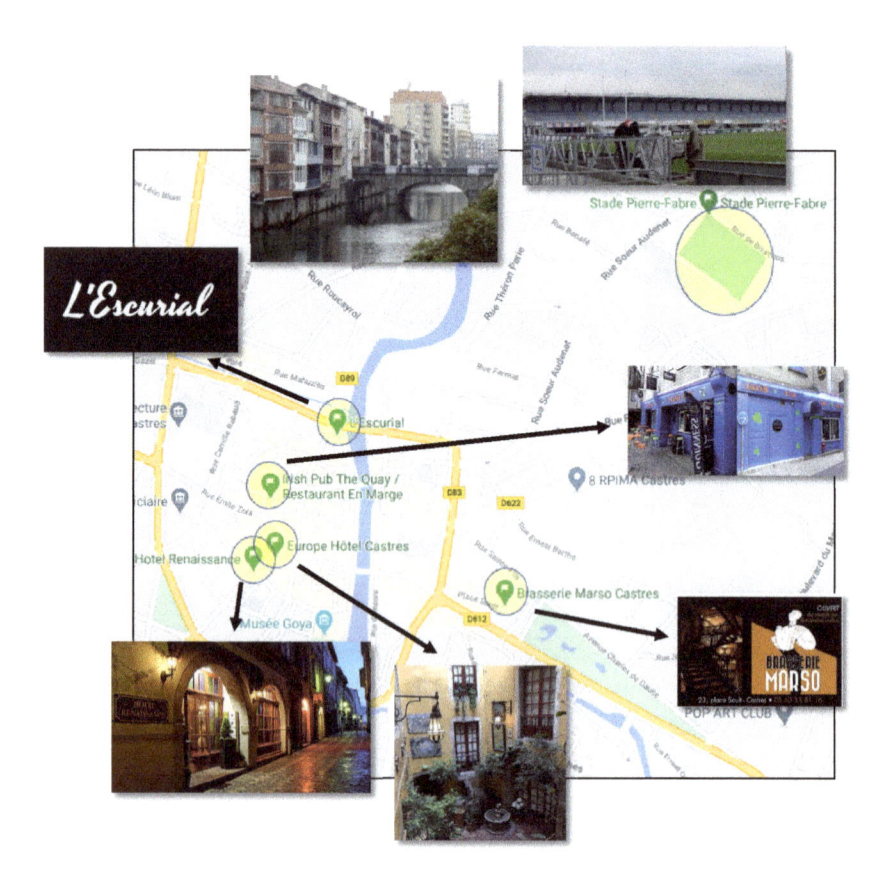

Highly Rated
- Hotel Renaissance
- Portofino

# Excursion from CASTRES - ALBI (TARN)

| CLUBNAME | S C Albi | STADIUM | Stadium Municipal d'Albi | | |
|---|---|---|---|---|---|
| ADDRESS | 283 Avenue Colonel Tessier, 81000 Albi | | | | |
| WEBSITE | www.sca.albi.fr | | | CAPACITY | 13,058 |

Albi is a second tier french team so it is unlikely that they will feature in the European competitions but it is well worth a visit.

We visited it from Castres it being 40 miles north of the Top 14 side and our return flight from Toulouse was south west on the motorway.

# CLERMONT FERRAND

| CLUBNAME | Clermont Auvergne | STADIUM | Parc de Marcel Michelin | |
|---|---|---|---|---|
| ADDRESS | Rue du Clos Four 63000 Clermont Ferrand Puy-de-Dome ||||
| WEBSITE | www.asm-rugby.com || CAPACITY | 18,030 |

Clermont boast the enthusiastic crowd in the Top 14. The passionate yellow army regularly contribute towards a winning formula which leads to a home record that is second to none. The success of Clermont is testament to the investment by their owners Michelin.

# GRENOBLE

| CLUBNAME | FC Grenoble | STADIUM | Stade Lesdiguieres |
|---|---|---|---|
| ADDRESS | Rue Albert Renier, 38100, Grenoble, Isere |||
| WEBSITE | www.fcgrugby.com | CAPACITY | |

Grenoble now play larger crowds at Stade des Alpes

Grenoble boasts an impressive modern ground to go with their history of alpine sports. The new ground (Stade de Alpes) unfortunately is not matched by the rugby results.

# LYON

| CLUBNAME | Lyon O U | STADIUM | Matmut | |
|---|---|---|---|---|
| ADDRESS | 8 Rue Oradour-sur-Glame, Lyon | | | |
| WEBSITE | www.lourugby.fr | | CAPACITY | 8,000 |

Lyon's Matmut stadium is now a rugby stadium the football having moved to a impressive new stadium, but the atmosphere at the rugby ground still generates a winning environment.

The ground is reached by the modern metro, the Blue Line will take you straight to Stade de Gerland.

Lyon is the gastronomic capital of France with hundreds of resturants around the impressive square Place Bellecour. On the high ground surrounding the historic part of Lyon is the awe inspiring Cathedral Saint-Jean-Baptiste de Lyon.

# MONTPELLIER (HERAULT)

| CLUBNAME | Montpellier | STADIUM | Altred Stadium |
|---|---|---|---|
| ADDRESS | 500 Avvenue de Vanieres, 34000, Montpellier, Herault | | |
| WEBSITE | www.montpellier-rugby.com | CAPACITY | 14,700 |

Montpellier is a beautiful city with an abundance of bars, cafes and historic buildings.

**Getting there** – Montpellier airport has direct flights to Luton, Gatwick and Leeds/Bradford. Transfers to city hotels are quick and frequent and with a fair wind you could transfer, check into your hotel and line up your first beer within an hour of your plane landing. TIP – book your flights early for lowest cost and availability

The magnificent Altred rugby stadium holds 16,000 so getting tickets is easy – buy online at the Montpellier website.

For a change of scene a trip to Sète for fresh sea air and seafood in a classy resort.

# PARIS

| CLUBNAME | Racing 92 | STADIUM | Stade Olympique Yves-du-Manoir | |
|---|---|---|---|---|
| ADDRESS | Colombes, Hauts-de-Seine | | | |
| WEBSITE | www.racing92.fr | | CAPACITY | 14,000 |

| CLUBNAME | Stade Francais | STADIUM | Stade Jean-Bouin | |
|---|---|---|---|---|
| ADDRESS | 20-40 Avenue du General Sarrall, 75000 Paris | | | |
| WEBSITE | www.stade.fr | | CAPACITY | 20,000 |

for bigger matches - Stade de France

The choice of resturants, bars and hotels is so plentiful for bigger matches - Stade de Franceou choose your own. The directions to the rugby grounds are well documented and easy to get to.

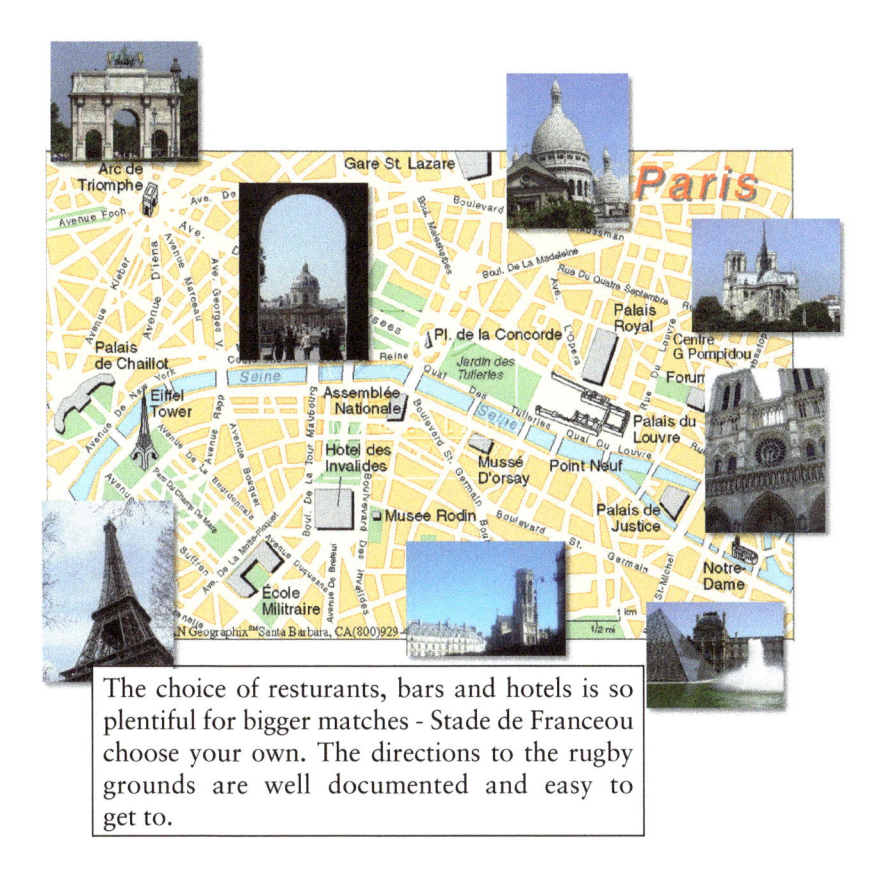

# PERPIGNAN (PYRENEES-ORIENTALES)

| CLUBNAME | USA Perpignan | STADIUM | Stade Aime Giral | | |
|---|---|---|---|---|---|
| ADDRESS | 11 Aime Giral, 66000, Perpignan | | | | |
| WEBSITE | www.usap.cat | | | CAPACITY | 14,593 |

### A TRUE STORY

In January 2009 we arranged a trip to Montpellier. Unfortunately TV changed schedule from Friday to Thursday. Not wanting to be denied live rugby we noted that down the coast Ospreys were due to play Perpignan. We got tickets in the "bear pit", a section of the ground for animals to stand and do a lot of the singing. We had decided to wear our Saints shirts which turned out to be a good decision because unbeknown to us Perpignan hate Montpellior and us beating them the previous night elevated us to hero status. That evening after the match free drinks and warm hand shakes were on offer whichever bar we ventured into.

# Excursions from Perpignan

## A) Eastern Pyrenees

A great excursion from Perpignan is to explore the eastern Pyrenees. The route is fairly straight forward; you just follow the N116 driving SW out of Perpignan. There are plenty of interesting villages but of particular note is Vernet-les-Bains, Villafranche, Mont Louis and Font-Romeu reaching a height of 1431 metres at Col-du-Chioule. The views from there are quite magnificent on a clear day.

From there you have a choice – you can either retrace your steps back to Perpignan (which would be a round trip of 200km) or do what we did and drive the 50km on to Andorra.

If your team includes keen skiers, then they could squeeze in half a day on the slopes as the route takes you very close to the piste at Solden. The following day we had a leisurely drive back to Carcassonne airport via the N20, D613, D118 which is approximately 150km. On the journey you will have fantastic views at Col-du-Chioule (height of 1431metres) and pass through the delightful town of Aix-les-Thermes, Quillan, and Limoux.

**Special Lunch** – At Vernet-les-Bains there is a restaurant called Bistrot Le Cortal. It is run by Tiffany and David Smith originally from Yorkshire. You are sure of a warm welcome, great food and stunning scenery.

## B) Collioure

This excursion is ideal for half a day. It is approximately 100km and is well worth the trip. The route is also straight forward – just follow the N114 south from Perpignan.

Collioure is a Mediterranean port near the Catalan border with Spain.

There is a dramatic and inspiring conflict between the ramparts of the old castle alongside quiet and quaint back streets where you can pick up some original crafts (as a peace offering if you need one). Aim to get there mid-morning and enjoy a fresh coffee in a beach cafe and people-watch.

Why not make a full day of it and after Collioure drive 10km south to Cebere, a small port on the French side with Port Bou 3km south on the Spanish side. If the weather is okay you can walk along the clifftop path to the Spanish side.

After a light Spanish lunch with a bottle of Rjoca, catch the train through the tunnel from Port Bou back to your car in Cebere.

# TOULON

| CLUBNAME | RC Toulonnais | STADIUM | Stade Mayol |
|---|---|---|---|
| ADDRESS | Quai, Lafontan, Toulon, Var | | |
| WEBSITE | www.rcloulon.com | CAPACITY | 15,400 |

Toulon came to the fore in French and European rugby with the help of a serious financial investor and the French "no ceiling" approach to recruitment Conseqently they built a team of super stars. They play at Stade Mayol which is situated next to the harbour and a road goes under the ground.

There is plenty to do and places to go. A trip to Marseille is worth doing. Catch a train.

Toulon is the naval port for France and you can take a boat trip around the destroyers and frigates. Behind Toulon is a mountain which is serviced by a cable car. The views from the top are breathtaking.

## Excursion from TOULON – MARSEILLE

A short train journey from Toulon takes you into the heart of Marseille. Wandering around the historic buildings is the perfect preparation for lunch overlooking the colourful harbour, basking In sunshine (in mid January) with a pint or 2.

## NICE

| CLUBNAME | Rugby Nice | STADIUM | Stade des Arboras |
|---|---|---|---|
| ADDRESS | 247 Route de Grenoble 062000, Nice. Cote d'Azur |||
| WEBSITE | www.stadenicols.fr | CAPACITY | 3,000 |

Nice Rugby currently play in the third tier in French rugby – so why include it in this book?

Well the reason is Nice was the first trip we made in 1998 and we won it 21-10. Also Nice is a lovely place and a 15 minute train journey takes you to Monte Carlo.

The principles we set out were –

1) Affordable – Value for money
2) Flexible – Practical and well planned

# TOULOUSE

| CLUBNAME | Stade Toulousain | STADIUM | Stade Ernest-Wallon |
|---|---|---|---|
| ADDRESS | 114 Rue des Troenes 31200 Toulouse, Haute-Garonne |||
| WEBSITE | www.stadetoulousain.fr | CAPACITY | 19,500 |

Toulouse is the third largest city in France (After Paris and Marsilles). It is a cultural and a technological centre hence the presence of Airbus Industries. The university is one of the largest in France. Toulouse is sometimes known as the Red City on account of the predominence of red brick buildings

The city is home to two rugby clubs - Stade Toulousain who play in the Top 14 league and Colomiers Rugby who play in the PRO DIV 2 League. Both share the Ernest Wallon stadium for their home games. The big fixtures are often scheduled to be played at the much larger football stadium. The stadium is located near the airport quite some distance out. Make sure you plan your journey back to city – it's a long walk.

Back at the city there are numerous bars and restauants. Start in Place Wilson but don't forget to visit Mr Brennen (ex Irish international player) who owns the best Irish bar.

Highly Rated
- Brennen's bar
- Frog & Rosbef

# Excursions from TOULOUSE –

## A) CARCASSONNE

| CLUBNAME | U S Carcassonne | STADIUM | Stade Albert Domec |
|---|---|---|---|
| ADDRESS | 32 Rue Antoine, 11000 Carcassonne | | |
| WEBSITE | www.uscarcassonne.com | CAPACITY | 11,000 |

Take a train from the central station in Toulouse to Carcassonne. There you will find an immaculate hillfort - Carcassonne are a 2$^{nd}$ tier rugby team frequently striving for promotion to TOP 14.

## B) CITE DE L'ESPACE

Take Metro line A to Jolimont then Bus 37.

# SPAIN

## SAN SEBASTIAN

It seems strange to include this Spanish city but being so close to Biarritz they have hosted several key fixtures at their 30,000 seater football ground. The town is full of historic and picturesque buildings and there are some fine restaurants and bars.

Regarding hotels you have two practical venues – San Sebastian or Bilbao.

We flew into Bilbao with Easyjet, stayed at the Petit Palace Arana and hired a car to get to the match.

## BILBAO – GUGGENHEIM MUSEUM

# ITALY

## PARMA

| CLUBNAME | Zebra | STADIUM | Stadio Sergio Lanfranchine | |
|---|---|---|---|---|
| ADDRESS | via del Popolo, Parma | | | |
| WEBSITE | www.zebrerugby.eu | CAPACITY | 5,000 | |

Parma is renowed for its refined social life. There are numerous theatres and restaurants. The culinary tradition stems from the local production of wonderful food products - Palma Ham and Parmesan cheese factories are numerous and most of them promote factory tours and sampling sessions.

There are museums featuring famous works of art from Antilami to Corrggio and Bodoni to Verdi. Of course we can match that with Carlsberg to Church's and Avon Cosmetics to Travis Perkins.

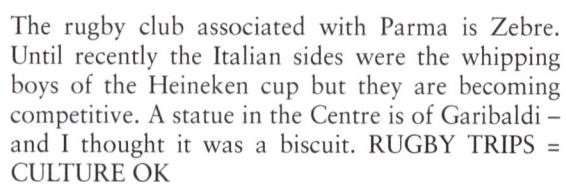

The rugby club associated with Parma is Zebre. Until recently the Italian sides were the whipping boys of the Heineken cup but they are becoming competitive. A statue in the Centre is of Garibaldi – and I thought it was a biscuit. RUGBY TRIPS = CULTURE OK

Highly Rated
- La Filoma

# TREVISO

| CLUBNAME | Benetton Treviso | STADIUM | Stadio comunale Monigo |
|---|---|---|---|
| ADDRESS | Strada di Nasimban 1/B 31100 Treviso |||
| WEBSITE | www.benettonrugby.it | CAPACITY | 6,700 |

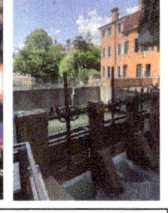

Treviso are arguably the best rugby team in Italy, but the city frequently gets snow. On one occasion we had to dig out the ground following a freak snow fall. Sitting on concrete steps was invigorating. For the keen skiers the Dolomite ski resorts are an hours drive north of Treviso. A day trip to Venice is worth doing but don't ignore the historic buildings of Treviso itself.

# EXCURSION FROM TREVISO – VENICE

If you have never been there Venice is a must visit if your schedule allows, but be aware it is more romantic in summer than the winter. You however might get a sunny day – we were blessed the day we visited mid-January as these pictures show.

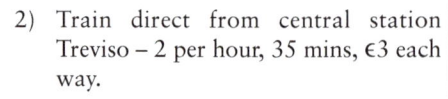

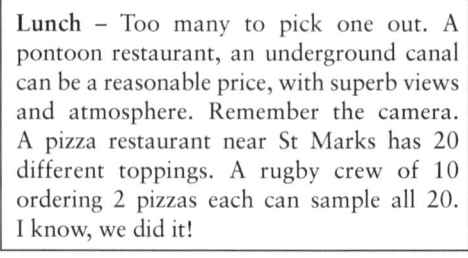

**Getting there** – there are 3 permutations:

1) If you have a car – drive it.
2) Train direct from central station Treviso – 2 per hour, 35 mins, €3 each way.
3) Bus – regular service from central bus station similar to train but 55 mins.

**Lunch** – Too many to pick one out. A pontoon restaurant, an underground canal can be a reasonable price, with superb views and atmosphere. Remember the camera. A pizza restaurant near St Marks has 20 different toppings. A rugby crew of 10 ordering 2 pizzas each can sample all 20. I know, we did it!

# VERONA / VIADANA

Viadana is a small town near Verona and is not an ideal venue for a rugby trip. As it happened the match was called off due to thick fog and therefore the trip became a cultural weekend in Verona. Verona proved to be an excellent host with two Irish bars and numerous high quality restaurants.

We stayed at The Grand Hotel, which is a quality four star hotel a short walk from the center of the city.

# IRELAND

## BELFAST

| CLUBNAME | Ulster Rugby | STADIUM | Kingspan Stadium |
|---|---|---|---|
| ADDRESS | 65 Ravenhill Road, Belfast, Northern Ireland |||
| WEBSITE | www.ulsterrugby.com | CAPACITY | 18,196 |

The best hotel in Belfast is the 4-star Hilton (there are deals to be done on a B&B basis). The Crown Bar is a must for a pint. The ground is now know as the Kingspan Stadium formally called Ravenhill Stadium.

## GALWAY

| CLUBNAME | Connacht Rugby | STADIUM | Galway Sports Grounds |
|---|---|---|---|
| ADDRESS | College Road, Galway, Elrel H91 H340 |||
| WEBSITE | www.connachtrugby.ie | CAPACITY | 9,500 |

# DUBLIN

| CLUBNAME | Leinster Rugby | STADIUM | Donnybrok |
|---|---|---|---|
| ADDRESS | 4 Donnybrook Road, Dublin 4 | | |
| WEBSITE | www.leinsterrugby.ie | CAPACITY | 6,000 |

Big matches are played at the Aviva Stadium

Dublin represents the ultimate in European club rugby weekends - it ticks most of the boxes. There are flights from many European cities - you can even take the car by ferry and use as a launchpad into Eire (the golf is very special).

There are hotels to suit most budgets with restaurants/bars serving excellent food and live music until the early hours.

But the atmosphere at the rugby is second to none – its intimidating and friendly even if Leinster lose (which is rare).

An evening in Temple Bar is a celebration of the "black stuff."

# EXCURSIONS FROM DUBLIN

## A) HOWTH & MALAHIDE

Take the DART train north and choose whether to do Malahide first or Howth. A lot will depend on where you decide to have lunch. A walk along the sea wall at Howth is worth doing – there is always activity in the vibrant fishing port to provide interest and the narrow streets leading from the quayside have some interesting shops.

At Malahide there is magnificent castle, grounds and a modern yacht marina.

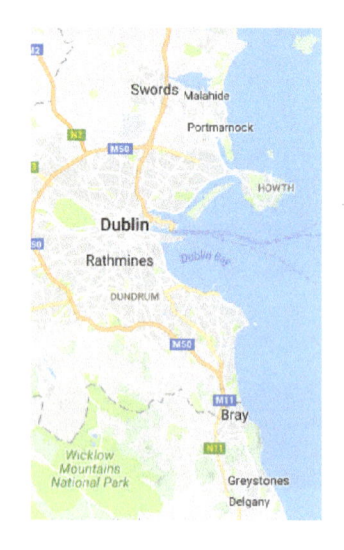

## B) GREYSTONES & BRAY

If the weather is half decent take a DART train south to Greystones and do the coastal walk north back to Bray. The walk is approximately 5 miles but despite being largely on top of the cliff the walk is relatively level.

The scenery is fantastic and the fresh air will give you an appetite on your return by train to Dublin.

For your achievement of completing the walk you need to award yourself an ice cream from the café on the sea front.

WHEN THE SAINTS GO MARCHING ABROAD

Greystones    Coastal Path    Bray

# LIMERICK

| CLUBNAME | Munster Rugby | STADIUM | Thomand Park | |
|---|---|---|---|---|
| ADDRESS | Cratloe Road, Limerick, Eire | | | |
| WEBSITE | www.munsterrugby.ie | CAPACITY | 25,630 | |

Munster Rugby is at the heart of Limerick life and no more so than to be in Clohessy's bar on match day.

We arrived in Limerick after an early morning flight from Coventry and felt it proper to get into the swing with 'The Works' -Full Irish Breakfast + Pint of Guiness at 9.00am.

There is much to see and do in Limerick plus a couple of worthwhile excursions.

The new stadium is very impressive and has the traditional Thomand Park atmosphere.

# Excursions from Limerick –
## A) Bunratty Castle

On the bus route to Shannon Airport, about ten miles north of Limerick, is the wonder of Bunratty Castle. A well preserved castle which is used for medieval banquets, in the grounds are a history lesson in life gone past.

For those of you not too fragile from the night before, you can climb the many steps to the ramparts of the castle and admire the splendid views across the Shannon estuary.

The historic village not surprisingly has a pub (yes its true they too have an Irish bar). In addition to some timely refreshment they have a good selection of home cooked food.

Allow about two hours for the visit – you will not be disappointed.

## B) Tour of S.W. Eire - Rock Castle, Killarney, and Dingle

### Distances

| Limerick | Adare | 20km |
| Limerick | Tralee | 100km |
| Tralee | Dingle | 50km |
| Killarney | Dingle | 65km |
| Killarney | Limerick | 120km |

### Ring of Kerry (optional extra)

# SCOTLAND

## GLASGOW

| CLUBNAME | Glasgow Warriors | STADIUM | Scotstoun Stadium |
|---|---|---|---|
| ADDRESS | 72 Danes Drive, Glasgow. G14 9HD | | |
| WEBSITE | www.glasgowwarriors.org | CAPACITY | 9,708 |

Glasgow Warriors are an up-and-coming team that play at the Scotstoun Stadium which is on the west side of the city. To get to the stadium you need to catch a train from central station and there is a five minute walk from the station.

The easiest way to get to Glasgow is by British Rail. A night out in Glasgow is an interesting experience. Of course a good night out is not complete without a deep fried Mars bar.

# EDINBURGH

| CLUBNAME | Edinburgh Rugby | STADIUM | BT Murrayfield |
|---|---|---|---|
| ADDRESS | Roseburn, Edinburgh. EH12 5PJ | | |
| WEBSITE | www.edinburghrugby.org | CAPACITY | 67,144 |

Edinburgh Rugby, formerly Reivers, play their home games at Murrayfield. Edinburgh is a spectacular city culminating in the famous castle and Holyrood Palace. As with Glasgow, a night out in Edinburgh is worth doing. It is a pity that the rugby calender does not include August otherwise your trip would include the 'Fringe'.

# WALES

## CARDIFF

| CLUBNAME | Cardiff Blues | STADIUM | Cardiff Arms Park |
|---|---|---|---|
| ADDRESS | Cardiff Arms Park, West Gate Street, Cardiff. CF10 1JA |||
| WEBSITE | www.cardiffblues.com | CAPACITY | 12,125 |

Cardiff Blues play their home fixtures at Cardiff Arms Park. Their stadium is in the shadow of the Principality Stadium but it still manages to host European Conference Finals. Cardiff are the inaugural runners-up of the Heineken Cup.

## NEWPORT

| CLUBNAME | Newport/Gwent Dragons | STADIUM | Rodney Parade |
|---|---|---|---|
| ADDRESS | Newport, Gwent, NP 19 0UU |||
| WEBSITE | www.newportgwentdragons.com | CAPACITY | 8,800 |

Dragons share ground with Newport County football club. In 2017 they changed the name of the club so now they are just known as Dragons.

# SWANSEA

| CLUBNAME | Ospreys Rugby | STADIUM | Liberty Stadium | | |
|---|---|---|---|---|---|
| ADDRESS | Landore Swansea. SA1 2FA | | | | |
| WEBSITE | www.ospreysrugby.com | | CAPACITY | 20,520 | |

| CLUBNAME | Llanelli Scarlets | STADIUM | Parc y Scarlets | | |
|---|---|---|---|---|---|
| ADDRESS | Parc Pemberton, Llanelli, Wales SA14 9UZ | | | | |
| WEBSITE | www.scarlets.co.uk | | CAPACITY | 14,870 | |

Swansea and Llaneli are geographically adjacent and as such can be covered as one. Swansea has the far superior night life.

**Getting there** – No major airport (Bristol and Cardiff nearest) therefore drive or better still go by train. Terrific deals to be done (including First Class ) by rail i.e. best seats, complimentary drinks and food.

**Match day** – both stadiums are modern and as such have great seats, good vision, reasonable price beer & food. However allow time to get to stadiums – both are out of town but a £5 taxi fare is well worth it, Ticketing is easy – their website is friendly and you can choose seats. Health tip for the morning after - walk around the docks and Swansea Bay or drive around Gower Peninsula.

WHEN THE SAINTS GO MARCHING ABROAD

# ENGLAND

# EXETER

| CLUBNAME | Exeter Chiefs | STADIUM | Sandy Park |
|---|---|---|---|
| ADDRESS | Sandy Park Way, Exeter. EX2 7NN | | |
| WEBSITE | www.exeterchiefs.co.uk | CAPACITY | 12,500 |

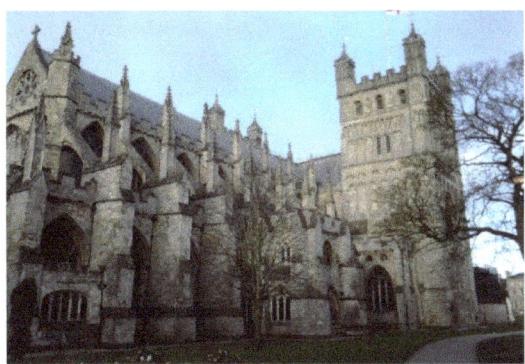

The most exciting development in European Rugby is the development of Exeter Rugby Club. From their base in Sandy Park, they have grown into a formidable unit that has launched them to European champions.

Exeter city is a blend of historical buildings and restaurants, ideal for a walk about before lunch.

## MANCHESTER

| CLUBNAME | Sale Sharks | STADIUM | A J Bell Stadium |
|---|---|---|---|
| ADDRESS | 1 Stadium Way, Eccles, Salford. M30 7EY | | |
| WEBSITE | www.salesharks.com | CAPACITY | 12,000 |

## LEEDS

| CLUBNAME | Yorkshire Carnegie | STADIUM | Headingley Stadium |
|---|---|---|---|
| ADDRESS | Headingley, Leeds | | |
| WEBSITE | www.leedsrugby.com | CAPACITY | 21,062 |

## NEWCASTLE

| CLUBNAME | Newcastle Falcons | STADIUM | Kingston Park |
|---|---|---|---|
| ADDRESS | Brunton Road, Newcastle, NE13 8AF | | |
| WEBSITE | www.newcastefalcons.co.uk | CAPACITY | 10,200 |

## PLYMOUTH

| CLUBNAME | Plymouth Albion | STADIUM | Brickfields |
|---|---|---|---|
| ADDRESS | Demarel Close, Plymouth, Devon | | |
| WEBSITE | www.plymouthalbion.com | CAPACITY | 6,500 |

Although technically all grounds in the top two divisions are reachable without an overnight stay, it would be a shame to miss out on an educational night out e.g. Studying the antics of the Geordie Hen Night Out (from a safe distance). It never ceases to amaze me that a stretch limo can transport so many office admin staff. They come in all shapes and sizes, many with inappropriate attire but all well oiled. They hunt in packs and do not take prisoners.

Above I suggest cities which warrant a stay.

Plymouth is quite a trek but be careful of the 2 for1 offer in the Walkabout Bar but recommend the All You Can Eat Chinese.

# PENZANCE/ST. IVES

| CLUBNAME | Cornish Pirates | STADIUM | Mennaye Field |
|---|---|---|---|
| ADDRESS | Penzance/Newlyn Rugby, Alexander Rd. Penzance TR18 4IY |||
| WEBSITE | www.cornish-pirates.com | CAPACITY | 4,000 |

You are probably wondering why the next three clubs are in this book that are not in the Premier League. Well with promotion and relegation and provided you are still enthusiastic in following your club and if you apply yourself to a UK weekend you can get as much pleasure out of visiting these championship teams. One day any one of them could do an "Exeter" and not only gain promotion, but secure a place at the top table and immediatly find themselves competing in Europe initially in the Challenge Cup. As I write this I am realising that the supporters of these teams have a new focus and need a copy of this book to guide and reassure them.

The first of this trio is Cornish Pirates who are based in Cornwall and have been consistently achieving top half of the Championship league for a decade. Their supporters are great fun – the banter on the sidelines is sublime with cutting comments and good humoured digs and they embrace all the positive attributes of rugby.

You should have little problem getting tickets – try their website (for the best seats and maybe avoid the handlng charge). They use two grounds – the one at Penzance and the Recreation Ground at Cambourne. They were also planning a new stadium at Truro.

On the way down to Cornwall there are several interesting places to visit. In particular I recommend –

a) The Eden project at St. Austell
b) Nearby Charleston Harbour – 2/3 good pubs for lunch
c) Truro with its magnificent cathedral
d) The coastal walk to Lands End

# Chapter 8

# Lions, Six Nations & World Cup

This is the big league and hence for it to be within the scope of this book we have to define the parameter –

The trip does not involve financial gain to the organiser.

The trip involves at least one overnight, a flight/train and match tickets.

Maximum participants – 8 which is 4 twin rooms or 2 taxis.

## The Lions Tours

This can be the trip of a lifetime provided you recognise the unique features and plan them into your itinerary carefully.

- Lions tours take place every four years and in turn involve New Zealand, Australia and South Africa
- The recent tours are 2009 South Africa, 2013 Australia, 2017 New Zealand
- The forth coming tours are 2021 South Africa and 2025 Australia

The British and Irish Lions consist of the best players from England, Wales, Scotland, Northern Ireland and Eire – a unique and unusual combination of culture, creed and character that somehow works for six weeks before they reform into their country teams for the next four years – the players and 40,000 supporters being united under the famous red shirts.

The last three Saturdays are the Test Matches. You would definitely want to include at least one of these in your itinerary.

## Six Nations

This is the top country competition for the northern hemisphere

The six countries that compete annually are:

| ENGLAND | FRANCE | WALES |
| SCOTLAND | ITALY | IRELAND |

They play each other once alternating between Home and Away so that one year they play 2 at home 3 away and the following year 3 at home and 2 away.

The teams are made up of the best players eligible to represent that country and are played January to March at the following stadiums –

### Twickenham, London - 82,000

## BT Murrayfield, Edinburgh – 67,144

## Aviva, Dublin - 51,700 (ex Lansdown Road)

WHEN THE SAINTS GO MARCHING ABROAD

## Principality, Cardiff – 74,500 ( ex Millennium)

## Stade de France, Paris – 80,698

## Stadio Olimpico, Rome – 73,261

## The World Cup

This is held every four years and can be in any country that plays rugby. By definition every match is an away match except for the host.

There are usually twenty countries structured into four groups of five with an element of seeding with the top two progressing to the quarter finals.

Previous locations –   2019 Japan

2015 England

2011 New Zealand

# Chapter 9

# French Top 14 yet to be visited

## BRIVE

| CLUBNAME | C A Brive | STADIUM | Stade Amedee Domench | |
|---|---|---|---|---|
| ADDRESS | 11 Avenue du 11 November 1948,19100,Brive-la-Galliarde | | | |
| WEBSITE | www.cabrive-rugby.ycom | CAPACITY | | 16,000 |

Brive were runners up the 2013 season

## LA ROCHELLE

| CLUBNAME | Atlantique Stade Rochelase | STADIUM | Marcelet Deflandre | |
|---|---|---|---|---|
| ADDRESS | 27 Avenue du Marcelet Juin, 17000 La Rochelle | | | |
| WEBSITE | www.staderochelaise | CAPACITY | | 15,000 |

Top 14 winners 2017 plus Pro D2 runners up in 2014 and 2010

## PAU

| CLUBNAME | Section Paloise | STADIUM | Stade du Hameau | |
|---|---|---|---|---|
| ADDRESS | Boulevard du l'aviation 64,000, Pau | | | |
| WEBSITE | www.sectionpalois.com | CAPACITY | | 13,819 |

Pro D2 winner and promoted to Top 14

# FRENCH PRO Div.2)

## STADE AURILLACOIS (CANTAL)

| CLUBNAME | Stade Aurillacois | STADIUM | Stade Jean Alric |
|---|---|---|---|
| ADDRESS | 64 Boulevard Louis Dazier, 15000, Aurillac |||
| WEBSITE | www.stade-aurillacois.fr | CAPACITY | 10,000 |

Aurillac narrowly missed promotion to Top 14 finishing 3rd in season 2015-21016 behind Lyon and Bayonne. They were promoted from Federale 1 to Pro Div.1 in 2007.

## C S BOURGOIN- JALLIEU (HERAULT)

| CLUBNAME | Bourgoin Jallieu | STADIUM | Stade Pierre Rajon |
|---|---|---|---|
| ADDRESS | 73 Avenue Proeffeur Tixier, 38300 Bourgoin-Jallieu |||
| WEBSITE | www.csbj-rugby.fr | CAPACITY | 10,000 |

Although currently mid-table in French 2nd Division, BJ have had some success over the years. In 1997 they were 2nd in the French championship, in European Challenge cup they were winners in 1997 and runners up in 1999 and 2009 losing to Northampton Saints in the final.

## COLOMIERS RUGBY(HAUTE-GARONNE)

| CLUBNAME | U S Colomiers | STADIUM | Stade Michel Bendichou |
|---|---|---|---|
| ADDRESS | Driveway Briere, 31770, Colomiers |||
| WEBSITE | www.colomiers-rugby.com | CAPACITY | 11,000 |

Colomiers won the European Challenge Cup in 1997 and were runners up in the Heineken Cup in 1998. They were losing finalist in 2000 in the French Championship and winners of Federale 1 in 2005 and 2009. They are currently mid-table in the PRO DIV 2.

## BOURG-ET- BRESSEE

| CLUBNAME | USBPA | STADIUM | Marcel verchere Stade |
|---|---|---|---|
| ADDRESS | 11 Avenuedes Sports, 01000,Bourg-et-Bresse |||
| WEBSITE | www.usbourg.com | CAPACITY | 11,400 |

Runners up in 2016-2017 in PRO D2. Promoted to Top 14.

## U S DAX (LANDES)

| CLUBNAME | U S Dax | STADIUM | Stade Maurice Boyau |
|---|---|---|---|
| ADDRESS | 3 Boulevard Paul Lasaosa BP41 40103 Dax |||
| WEBSITE | www.usdax.fr | CAPACITY | 16,170 |

Dax have been in danger of relegation to Federale 1 for the past 2 seasons. In the past they have been runners up in the French Championship in 1956, 1961, 1963 and 1973. They have however won the French cup in 1956, 1957 and 1959.

## R C MASSY (ESSONNE)

| CLUBNAME | R C Massy Essonne | STADIUM | Stade de Jules Ladoumegue |
|---|---|---|---|
| ADDRESS | 8 Alec du Roussel.91300 Massy |||
| WEBSITE | www.rcmassone.com | CAPACITY | 3,200 |

Promoted to PRO D2 in 2016.

## STADE MONTOIS (LANDES)

| CLUBNAME | Stade Montois | STADIUM | Stade Guy Boniface |
|---|---|---|---|
| ADDRESS | 270 Avenue du Stade, 40000, Mont du Marsam |||
| WEBSITE | www.stademontoisrugby.fr | CAPACITY | 22,000 |

4th in PRO D2 in 2017.

## R C NARBONNE (AUDE)

| CLUBNAME | Racing Club Narbonne | STADIUM | Parc Des Sports de l'Amitie | | |
|---|---|---|---|---|---|
| ADDRESS | 5 Rue Guy Lussac.11100. Narbonne | | | | |
| WEBSITE | www.rcnm.fr | | | CAPACITY | 12,000 |

Finished 12th in PRO D2 in 2017.

## U S MONTAUBAN(TARN-ET-GARONNE)

| CLUBNAME | U S Montauban | STADIUM | Stade Sapiac | | |
|---|---|---|---|---|---|
| ADDRESS | 12 rue du Chanoine, 82000. Montauban | | | | |
| WEBSITE | www.usmsaplac.fr | | | CAPACITY | 12,600 |

Promoted to TOP 14 as Playoff Winner 2006.

## SOYAUX ANGOULEME(CHARENTE)

| CLUBNAME | Soyaux Angouleme | STADIUM | Stade Chanzy | | |
|---|---|---|---|---|---|
| ADDRESS | 5 Rue du Stade, 16000 Angouleme | | | | |
| WEBSITE | www.saxycharente.fr | | | CAPACITY | 5,000 |

Finished 13th PRO D2 in 2017.

## R C VANNES(MORBIHAN)

| CLUBNAME | R C Vannes | STADIUM | Stade de la Rabine | | |
|---|---|---|---|---|---|
| ADDRESS | 2 Avenue du 4 Aout 1944 56000, Vannes | | | | |
| WEBSITE | www.rugbvclubvannes.com | | | CAPACITY | 9,500 |

Finished 11th in PRO D2 in 2017.

# Chapter 10

# Top 10 Irish Bars

My team and I are convinced that in most of the rugby town/cities there is an Irish bar. We tend to head there as our first step in the rigorous training regime. Here are our top ten.

**1. Brennan's Bar, Toulouse**

12 Grand Place Castelignest 31780
www.brennansbar.fr
TEL. +33 5 62 22 80 93
Open

**2. The Quay, Castres**

23 Rue Frederic Thomas 81100
Tel - +33 5 63 71 91 80
www.hamaquay.com
Open – 4.00pm – 2.00pm

**3. Pub Mulligans, Biarritz**

4 Allee du Cadran 64600, Anglet
tel. +33 5 59 42 06 07
www.pub-mulligan.com
open – 10.30am – 12.30am

### ④ Fitzpatrick's Irish Pub Montpellier
5 Place Saint-Come, 34000
Tel. +33 4 67 60 58 30
www.fitzpatricksirishpub.com
Open 12pm -1am

### ⑤ Irish Tattoo Pub Toulon
Place Monsenegue 83000
Tel. +33 4 94 89 68 09
www.navy-irish-pub.fr.gd
Open – always

### ⑥ Irish Free State Pub Treviso
via Costello d'Amore 232531100
Tel +39 349 225 5454
www.
Open – 18.00pm – 02.00pm

### ⑦ Celtic Pub Verona
via Santa Chiara, 37129
+39 383 877 1783
www.facebook.com/celticpubv
Open 5.30pm – 2.00am-

## 8  O'Callaghans, Grenoble

2 Place de Barulle 38000,, Grenoble.
www.ocallaghans-grenoble.com
tel. +33 4 76 01 66
open 3pm – 12am

## 9  Molly Malone's, Bordeaux

83 Quai des Chatrons 33300
www.molly-pub.fr
+33 5 57 87 06 72
opening times  10.30am – 2.00am

## 10  TEMPLE BAR, DUBLIN
Not just a pub but a street of pubs

**GUINNESS**
ST JAMES'S GATE BREWERY, DUBLIN

A must do culminating in the 360 bar with magnificent views of Dublin

Black is beautiful

…..but actually it's red

# Chapter 11

# Memorable Occasions

**Best Match** – Quarter final Heineken cup 2007. The match was held over the Spanish border in the 30,000 football stadium in San Sebastian. Despite being massive underdogs the 29,000 French/Spanish supporters were silenced by the singing of the 1000 Saints supporters as the full time score was Biarritz 6 – Saints 7. In defeat they were very gracious and made us very welcome.

**Best Hotel** – Renaissance, Castres – very unusual private hotel run by Michel with every room uniquely furnished with artifacts from around the world.

**Best Weather** Paris October 2014 – cloudless skies and temperatures in the 70s enhanced the sightseeing around beautiful Paris.

**Best Meal** - Moroccan restaurant in Toulon- Huge portions and an explosion of flavours that was enjoyed by all.

**Best Value** – Unusually Glasgow 2015 – we stumbled on a weekend break deal that was excellent value – First Class rail from Milton Keynes to Glasgow with complementary food and drinks all the way, 2 nights bed and full Scottish breakfast at the 4-star Jury's Inn. All this for only £159.50 each.

**Overall Best Weekend** – Toulon 2008. Brilliant from the start. The match was on the Friday night – we won 56-3. Great hotel (3 nights). Day trip to Marseille in hot sunshine, tour by ferry of the naval base, ascent of the cliffs by cable car and first class food and drinks. Total cost all in £450.

# Chapter 12

# Post Trip Review and Report

Following every trip I seek feedback from the attendees as to what worked well and what was not so successful. The objective is to ensure we continue to learn and enhance future trips.

Only those aspects that we can control are helpful e.g. we cannot anticipate bad weather but we can be judged on our contingency plans.

The type of questions might be –

- Airport – journey to and from
- Car parking costs and time to reach terminal plus collection process and time waiting
- Flight carrier and time of departure
- Cost of flight
- Transport – airport to hotel – use of taxis vs airport/city coaches, frequency and cost
- Hotel –
    - Location – distance to city centre
    - Quality vs cost
    - Rooms size and layout
    - Beds - comfort/good kip-ability
    - Breakfast
    - Bar – open hours and ambience
    - Staff – friendly and helpful
    - Other amenities – e.g. swimming pool, car parking
    - Overall – would you recommend it

- Match tickets – cost vs position
- Getting to and from stadium
- Friendliness of away supporters pre, during and post match
- The degree of culture built into the trip
- The quantity of exercise crammed in between refreshment periods
- Any planned excursions – were they worth doing

External factors are outside our control but contribute massively to the success of the weekend include –

- The weather – rounds 5 & 6 are scheduled for mid-January
- The result of the match and possibly the quality of the match but after all a win is a win
- The referee – we try to help him but somehow, he takes more notice of home team supporters. To their credit they often have a beer in the bar after the match
- The exchange rate as measured in worldwide currency unit the POG (Pint of Guinness).

# Chapter 13

# Summary and Conclusions

Well, you now have the toolkit – it's time to put it into action. Such trips can bond a group together but could equally cause friction between friends if someone forgets to do a critical aspect.

As already mentioned, the organiser must ensure that members of the team honour their commitment to the trip and pay up as and when summonsed.

The data and information contained in this book is/was correct at the time of publishing to the best endeavours of the Author. However, it is intended to produce revised additions in the future.

Readers of the book are most welcome to provide corrections, additions and relevant new data. In particular, any contributions for the towns we haven't yet visited.

They should do so by sending the details as an attachment to –

peter.harling@nortonexecutive.com

Anyone who has their submission successfully included in a revised edition will receive a free copy of that edition.

# APPENDIX 1(a)

# Flight Options – Table 1

DESTINATION        UK DEPARTURE AIRPORT

| DESTINATION | | ABZ | BFS | BHX | BLA | BOH | BRI | CWL | DSA |
|---|---|---|---|---|---|---|---|---|---|
| **FRANCE** | | | | √ | | | | | |
| Bergerac | EGC | | | F | | | R | | |
| Beziers | BZR | | | | | | R | | |
| Biarritz | BIQ | | | F | | | | | |
| Bordeaux | BOD | | E | F | | | ER | | |
| Brive | BE | | | | | | | | |
| Carcassonne | CCF | | | | | | | | |
| Chambery | CMF | | | F | | | | F | |
| Grenoble | GNB | E | | | | | E | | |
| La Rochelle | LRH | | | F | | | | | |
| Lyon | LYS | E | | F | | | E | | |
| Marseille | MRS | | | | | | E | | |
| Montpellier | MPL | | | | | | | | |
| Nice | NCE | E | | | | | E | | |
| Nimes | FNI | | | F | | | | | |
| Paris | CDG | F | | F | | F | E | F | F |
| Perpignan | PGF | | F | R | | | | | |
| St.Etienne | EBU | | | | | | | | |
| Toulon-Hyeres | TLN | | | | | | | | |
| Toulouse | TLS | | | | | | E | F | |
| **ITALY** | | | | | | | | | |
| Verona | VRN | | | R | | | | | |
| Treviso | TSF | | | | | | R | | |
| Venice | VCE | | | | | | E | | |
| Bergamo | BGY | | | | | | R | | |
| Parma | PMF | | | | | | | | |
| **EIRE** | | | | | | | | | |
| Dublin | DUB | A | | RA | A | RA | RA | | A |
| Cork | ORK | | | A | | | A | | |
| Shannon | SNN | | | | | | | | |
| Kerry | KIR | | | | | | | | |

| | | | | |
|---|---|---|---|---|
| A | Aer Lingus | | ABZ | Aberdeen |
| B | British Airways | | BFS | Belfast Int. |
| E | Easyjet | | BHX | Birmingham |
| F | Flybe | | BLA | Blackpool |
| J | Jet 2 | | BOH | Bournemouth |
| R | Ryanair | | BRS | Bristol |
| | | | CWL | Cardiff |
| | | | DSA | Doncaster |

# APPENDIX 1(b)

# Flight Options – Table 2

DESTINATION       UK DEPARTURE AIRPORT

| | | LPL | LTN | MAN | NCL | NQY | SEN | SOU | STN |
|---|---|---|---|---|---|---|---|---|---|
| **FRANCE** | | | | | | | | | |
| Bergerac | EGC | R | | F | | | F | | |
| Beziers | BZR | | R | R | | | | | |
| Biarritz | BIQ | | | | | | | | R |
| Bordeaux | BOD | E | E | | | | | F | |
| Brive | BE | | | | | | | | R |
| Carcassonne | CCF | R | | R | | | | | R |
| Chambery | CMF | | | J | J | | | F | |
| Grenoble | GNB | E | E | J | | | | | E |
| La Rochelle | LRH | | | | | | | F | |
| Lyon | LYS | | E | EJF | | | E | F | |
| Marseille | MRS | | | E | | | | | R |
| Montpellier | MPL | | E | | | | | | |
| Nice | NCE | E | E | | E | | | | E |
| Nimes | FNI | | R | | | | | F | |
| Paris | CDG | E | | EF | | | E | | |
| Perpignan | PGF | | | | | | | | R |
| St.Etienne | EBU | | | | R | | | | |
| Toulon-Hyeres | TLN | | | | | | | | |
| Toulouse | TLS | | | J | R | | | F | R |
| **ITALY** | | | | | | | | | |
| Verona | VRN | | | | JR | | | | |
| Treviso | TSF | | | | | | | | |
| Venice | VCE | E | EJ | | | | E | | |
| Bergamo | BGY | | | | | | | | |
| Parma | PMF | | | | | | | | R |
| **EIRE** | | | | | | | | | |
| Dublin | DUB | | R | R | R | A | R | A | |
| Cork | CRK | R | | A | A | | | | |
| Shannon | SNN | | | | R | | | | |
| Kerry | KIR | | R | | | | | | |

|   |   |   |   |
|---|---|---|---|
| A | Aer Lingus | LPL | Liverpool |
| B | British Airways | LTN | Luton |
| E | Easyjet | MAN | Manchester |
| F | Flybe | NCL | Newcastle |
| J | Jet 2 | NQY | Newquay |
| R | Ryanair | SEN | Southend on Sea |
|   |   | SOU | Southampton |
|   |   | STN | Stansted |

# APPENDIX 1(c)
# Flight Options – Table 3

## DESTINATION — UK DEPARTURE AIRPORT

| DESTINATION | | LPL | LTN | MAN | NCL | NQY | SEN | SOU | STN |
|---|---|---|---|---|---|---|---|---|---|
| **FRANCE** | | | | | | | | | |
| Bergerac | EGC | R | | F | | | | F | |
| Beziers | BZR | | R | R | | | | | |
| Biarritz | BIQ | | | | | | | | R |
| Bordeaux | BOD | E | E | | | | | F | |
| Brive | BE | | | | | | | | R |
| Carcassonne | CCF | R | | R | | | | | R |
| Chambery | CMF | | | J | J | | | F | |
| Grenoble | GNB | E | E | J | | | | | E |
| La Rochelle | LRH | | | | | | | F | |
| Lyon | LYS | | E | EJF | | | E | F | |
| Marseille | MRS | | | E | | | | | R |
| Montpellier | MPL | | E | | | | | | |
| Nice | NCE | E | E | | E | | | | E |
| Nimes | FNI | | R | | | | | F | |
| Paris | CDG | E | | EF | | | E | | |
| Perpignan | PGF | | | | | | | | R |
| St.Etienne | EBU | | | | R | | | | |
| Toulon-Hyeres | TLN | | | | | | | | |
| Toulouse | TLS | | | J | R | | | F | R |
| **ITALY** | | | | | | | | | |
| Verona | VRN | | | | JR | | | | |
| Treviso | TSF | | | | | | | | |
| Venice | VCE | E | | EJ | | | E | | |
| Bergamo | BGY | | | | | | | | |
| Parma | PMF | | | | | | | | R |
| **EIRE** | | | | | | | | | |
| Dublin | DUB | | R | R | R | A | R | A | |
| Cork | ORK | R | | A | A | | | | |
| Shannon | SNN | | | R | | | | | |
| Kerry | KIR | | R | | | | | | |

| | | | |
|---|---|---|---|
| | | LPL | Liverpool |
| A | Aer Lingus | LTN | Luton |
| B | British Airways | MAN | Manchester |
| E | Easyjet | NCL | Newcastle |
| F | Flybe | NQY | Newquay |
| J | Jet 2 | SEN | Southend on Sea |
| R | Ryanair | SOU | Southampton |
| | | STN | Stansted |

# APPENDIX 2
# Northampton Saints Results in Europe

| Season | CUP | Group Stage ||||||  Knockout stage ||
|---|---|---|---|---|---|---|---|---|---|
| | | Team 1 | Score | Team 2 | Score | Team 3 | Score | Team | Score |
| 1998-99 | EC | Nice | 21-10 | Bordeaux | 16-23 | Connacht | 13-43 | | |
| 1999-00 | HC | Grenoble | 18-20 | Edinburgh | 37-08 | Neath | 39-23 | Llanelli SF | 31-29 |
| 2000-01 | HC | Biarritz | 30-37 | Leinster | 31-40 | Edinburgh | 15-18 | | |
| 2001-02 | HC | Montferand | 17-50 | Cardiff | 17-25 | Glasgow | 27-31 | | |
| 2002-03 | HC | Biarritz | 20-23 | Cardiff | 31-00 | Ulster | 13-16 | | |
| 2003-04 | HC | Agen | 19-06 | Scarlets | 09-41 | Borders | 29-09 | | |
| 2004-05 | HC | Toulouse | 12-25 | Scarlets | 22-20 | Glasgow | 13-09 | Toulouse QF | 9-37 |
| 2005-06 | HC | Narbonne | 32-20 | Bristol | 28-36 | Viadama | WO | | |
| 2006-07 | HC | Biarritz | 10-22 | Parma | 68-21 | Borders | 29-03 | Biarritz QF | 7-6 |
| 2007-08 | | No Europe - Played in Championship - Promoted |||||| | |
| 2008-09 | HC | Toulon | 56-3 | Montpellier | 28-24 | Bristol | 25-21 | | |
| 2009-10 | HC | Perpignan | 13-29 | Munster | 09-12 | Treviso | 21-18 | Munster QF | 19-33 |
| 2010-11 | HC | Castres | 40-24 | Cardiff | 23-19 | Edinburgh | 32-28 | Leinster F | 22-33 |
| 2011-12 | HC | Castres | 22-41 | Munster | 21-23 | Scarlets | 29-17 | | |
| 2012-13 | HC | Castres | 16-21 | Ulster | 10-09 | Glasgow | 20-27 | | |
| 2013-14 HCEC | | Castres | 13-19 | Ospreys | 29-17 | Leinster | 18-09 | Bath ECF | 30-16 |
| 2014-15 | HC | Racing 92 | 14-22 | Ospreys | 20-09 | Treviso | 38-15 | Clermont | 5-37 |
| 2015-16 | HC | Racing 92 | 03-33 | Scarlets | 22-10 | Glasgow | 26-15 | | |
| 2016-17 | HC | Leinster | 13-60 | Castres | 07-41 | Montpellier | 17-26 | | |
| 2017-18 | HC | Clermont | 07-21 | Ospreys | 15-32 | Saracens | 14-62 | | |
| 2018-19 | HC | Clermont | 40-48 | Newport | 35-21 | Timisoara | 28-00 | | |
| 2019-20 | HC | Leinster | 21-50 | Lyon | 25-14 | Treviso | 35-32 | Exeter QF | 15-38 |

| | | | |
|---|---|---|---|
| | Trip organized | HCEC | Started in HC, runners up into EC |
| | No overnight | HC | Heineken Cup |
| | No interest | EC | European Conference |

| Date | Achievements | | |
|---|---|---|---|
| May-00 | Winner HC | Last 12 Seasons | |
| Apr-05 | Quarter-Final HC | Played | 41 |
| Apr-07 | Semi-Final EC | Won | 20 |
| May-09 | Winner EC | Lost | 21 |
| Apr-10 | Quarter-Final HC | % Won | 0.49% |
| May-11 | Final HC | Trips | 27 |
| May-14 | Winner EC | % Attended | 66% |
| Oct-00 | Quarter-Final HC | | |

79

# APPENDIX 3

# Multiple Matches

| Played > once |   |    |
|---|---|---|
| Castres | 5 |  |
| Leinster | 4 | +1 |
| Scarlets | 4 |  |
| Clermont | 4 |  |
| Edinbugh | 3 |  |
| Glasgow | 3 |  |
| Treviso | 3 |  |
| Biarritz | 3 | +1 |
| Ospreys | 3 |  |
| Cardiff | 2 |  |
| Bristol | 2 |  |
| Borders | 2 |  |
| Munster | 2 | +1 |
| Ulster | 2 |  |
| Racing 92 | 2 |  |
| Montpellier | 2 |  |
|  | 46 | +3 |

| Played once |  |
|---|---|
| Nice |  |
| Grenoble |  |
| Agen |  |
| Toulon |  |
| Narbonne |  |
| Toulouse +1 |  |
| Perpignan |  |
| Bordeaux |  |
| Connacht |  |
| Saracens |  |
| Neath |  |
| Parma |  |
| Viadama (Verona) |  |
| Timisoara |  |
| 14 | 60 |

| Trips Arranged |   |
|---|---|
| Agen | 1 |
| Belfast | 2 |
| Biarritz | 4 |
| Bordeaux | 1 |
| Borders | 1 |
| Cardiff | 2 |
| Castres | 4 |
| Clermont | 1 |
| Connacht | 1 |
| Dublin | 4 |
| Edinburgh | 1 |
| Glasgow | 2 |
| Grenoble | 1 |
| Limerick | 3 |
| Lyon | 2 |
| Montpellier | 1 |
| Nice | 1 |
| Paris | 2 |
| Parma | 1 |
| Perpignan | 2 |
| Swansea | 1 |
| Timisoara | 1 |
| Toulon | 1 |
| Toulouse | 3 |
| Treviso | 1 |
| Verona | 1 |
| English trip | 6 |
| Venues | 51 |

# APPENDIX 4

# Grounds used for Rugby Union matches additional to those listed in Chapters 6-9

|  |  |  | Capacity |
|---|---|---|---|
| • | Marseille | Orange Velodrome, Marseille FC | 67,394 |
| • | Stade de France | National Stadium Paris | 81,338 |
| • | Toulouse | Stade Municipal | 33,000 |
| • | Leicester | King Power, Leicester City | 32,312 |
| • | Twickenham | England RFU | 82,000 |
| • | Murrayfield | Scottish RFU, Edinburgh | 67,144 |
| • | Dublin (1) | Irish National Stadium, Aviva | 51,700 |
| • | Dublin (2) | Dublin Showground | 18,500 |
| • | Milton Keynes | Stadium MK | 30,500 |
| • | Cardiff | Principality Stadium (ex Millenium) | 74,500 |